Fore

Welcome to Alec Wills' sec...
we're serving up a festive ...
We've gathered his delightful collection of original
watercolour Christmas cards—yes, the same
handmade gems he sent to his family and friends for
years.

Picture this: wise men looking a little too wise,
snowmen with more curiosity than your cat, and
Santa's reindeer, who are definitely overdue for a spa
day. Alec's creativity is bound to bring you a chuckle
(or two!) as you flip through this festive bumper
edition.

And because Alec didn't take a holiday even during
the lockdown, we've included a 'Bonus' section
featuring his COVID Collection—proof that not even a
pandemic could keep him from spreading cheer.

So go on, have a laugh, feel the Christmas spirit, and
enjoy the whimsical world of Alec Wills!

"Come on –throw it"

How did Mary and Joseph get their
Groceries deliverd ?
   On a Lidl donkey

I WONDER IF GREEN WOULD SUIT ME..?

NEXT APPOINTMENT, THE 25th

"WE GOT THE TREE FROM THE RECYCLING CENTRE."

Snowman picking his nose

"I can see you've been working out"

Three Wise Men

Bonus Selection

Alec Wills' Lockdown Collection

"Sorry we couldn't come earlier-we were in Lockdown ! "

NEW PREMIER LEAGUE "SOCK-ER" KIT

Happy Mothers Day

Just to be on the safe side

"I SEE YOU MANAGED TO GET SOME SELF RAISING FLOUR."

"I HAVE JUST FOUND A PENCIL"

HEY LITTLE HEN
WHEN, WHEN, WHEN.
WILL YOU LAY ME
AN EGG FOR MY TEA ?

" I'M LOOKING FOR MY BRA."

CARRI PLAYING HER 2-M
SOCIAL DISTANCING FLUTE.

"DAD, YOU SAID THAT WE WERE GOING TO A 'BAR-B-QUE.'"

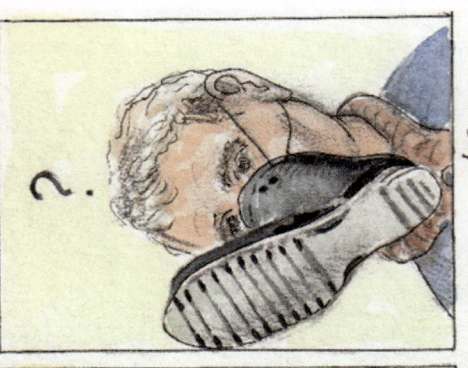

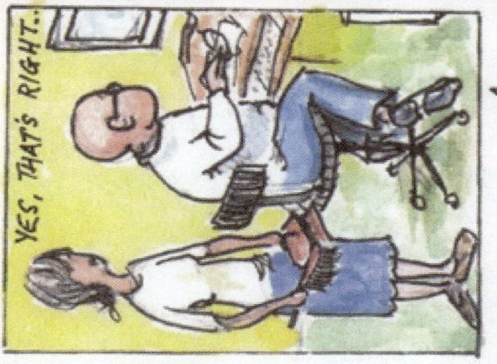

About the author and illustrator - Alec Wills
Alec Wills is married, with two stepchildren, three grandchildren and one great grandchild. He likes to paint local scenes of Poole in water colour, which he exhibits in local galleries. He also draws cartoons and illustrations for national and local magazines.

About The Publisher - Martyn Brown's Marketing Bugle

Marketing Bugle are digital marketing consultants for local businesses specialising in website builds, Email marketing systems, Social Media, Promotional videos and online marketing

First Published Sept. 2024
©2024 Marketing Bugle & Alec Wills Publications
Suite 4 The Triangle, Poole BH16 5PG
Inquiries: admin@marketingbugle.co.uk

Another available book featuring Alec J. Wills Illustrations

Children's Rhymes

by
Frank Horner

Step into the whimsical world of Frank Horner, an inspector for the RSPCA in the picturesque landscape of Dorset, UK. Although Frank's journey on this earth ended in 1989, his enchanting legacy lives on through the delightful rhymes he crafted with the dream of sharing them with children during their cherished reading-time moments.

THRUSH
Before Christmas, I ate rose hips so red,
Then holly berries and mistletoe, it's said.
They grow so high on elm tree tops,
Far from the reach of Christmas shops.
Searched the leaves and compost heap,
Singing a song so clear and sweet.
Sing and sing whatever the day,
Till I build my nest in a bush of May.

Scan for Website

Illustrations
Alec Wills

Printed in Great Britain
by Amazon